MW00611621

better together*

*This book is best read together, grownup and kid.

a
kids
book
about

a kids book about TRAUMA

by Megan Bartlett

a
kids
book
about

Printed in the United States of America.

A Kids Book About books are available online: *akidsco.com*

To share your stories, ask questions, or inquire about bulk purchases (schools, libraries, and nonprofits), please use the following email address: *hello@akidsco.com*

ISBN: 978-1-953955-10-4

Designed by Rick DeLucco
Edited by Denise Morales Soto

For Jack.

Trauma is a big, scary word. And it's normal to be a little overwhelmed when we think about how to help someone who's experienced trauma. Maybe we think we can't help at all because we aren't trained therapists or psychologists. But healing from trauma is about small interactions as much as (if not more than) big interventions. It's about connection and regulation, making sure we feel safe, and keeping our body rhythm in sync.

You are a healer. Really. You're a healer every time you become the trusted, caring grownup in a kid's (or anyone's) life. Every high five, every smile, every affirming moment of positive connection buffers us from the impact of overwhelming stress or trauma. Every time you encourage a kid to move their body, jam out to some music, or spend time bathing in the rhythms of the natural world, you put them on a path toward healing.

Healing is a team sport, and yes, sometimes we need professionals to be part of the team. But a caring, trusted grownup is nonnegotiable. Because connectedness is more powerful than adversity.

So, come on, healer. What are you waiting for?

Hi, I'm Megan.

Thank you for reading this book.

Before we get started,
I would like us to do an
activity together.

How does that sound?

Good, I hope!

So grab the grownup
reading this book with you and

Note: All of these exercises can
be done seated or standing.

As you go through them,
feel free to adjust as you go,
ask your grownup for help, and
do whatever works best for you!

First, I want you to reach up
as high as you can!

Put your arms up
and your head back,
and puff out your chest
as if you're reaching for the sun.

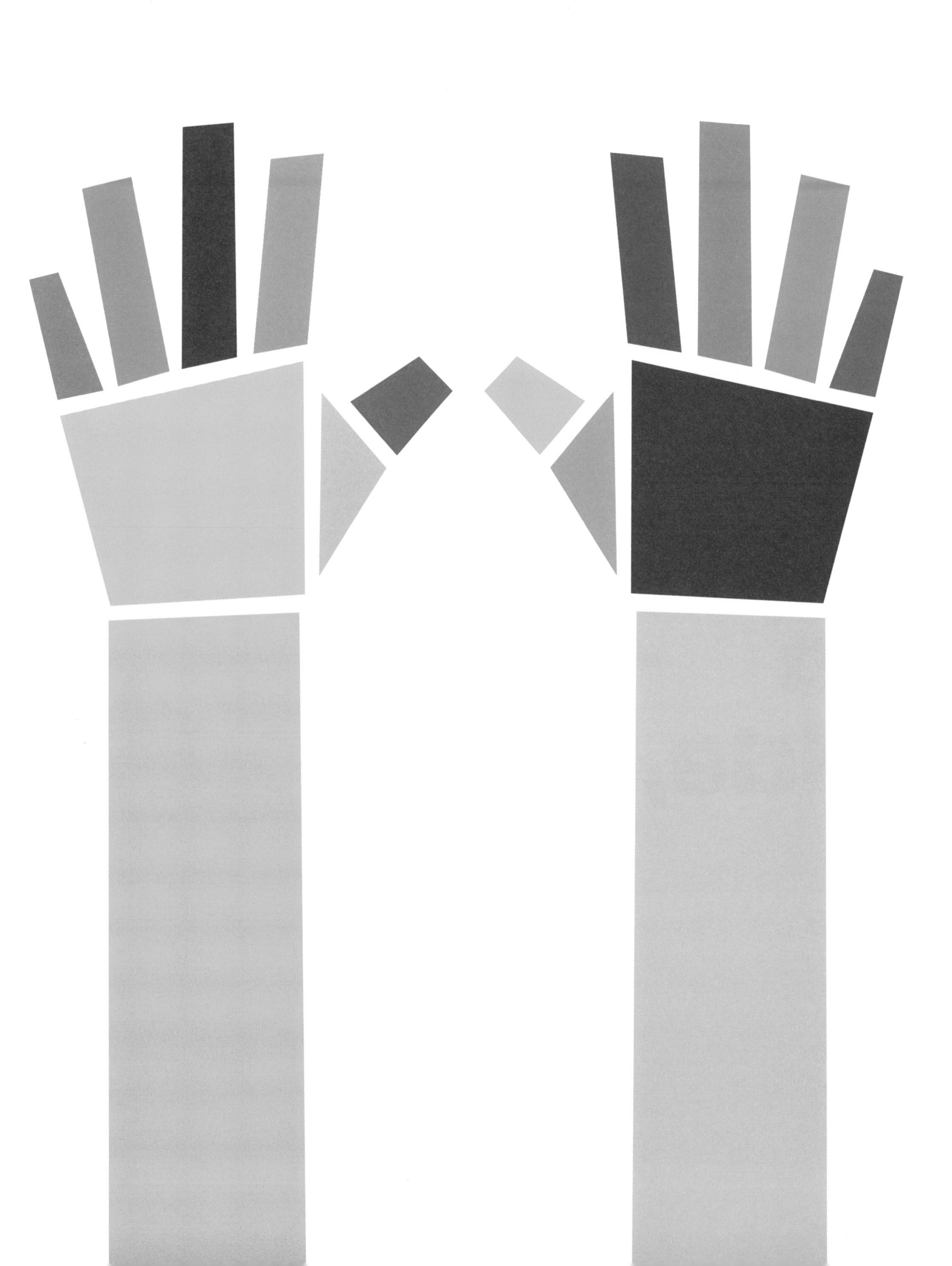

Now, with your arms in the air, sway back and forth,

side to side,

side
to
side.

Finally, let's get our heart rate up a little—let's jog in place, march, or pump your arms back and forth for 10 seconds.

Ready? GO!

OK, great!

Now that we’ve moved our
bodies and are all warmed up,
we’re ready to read this book.

You may be asking,
"Megan, why did I have to move my body before reading this book?"

Good question!

Moving our bodies—especially with those we love and care about—helps us feel safe, which is good for our brains.

When our brains feel safe,
we can learn more.

So now that we're all
warmed up, we're ready
to get into this book.

TRA

UMA

is a word you may have heard before.

We often hear it when we talk about going off to war, natural disasters, a school shooting, or abuse.

But did you know that
trauma can also be...

when a family might not have enough food for the week?

being really, really sick?

your parents getting divorced?

feeling different from everybody else and like you don't belong?

Because trauma isn't only
big, scary moments; trauma
is our body's reaction to
overwhelmingly stressful
experiences, and those can look
like a lot of different things.

Interesting,

Let me explain a little more.

Our brains are in charge of how we respond to stress.*

*Stress is how your mind and body react to the difficult things that happen in your life.

Think about the
first day of school.

**It can
be kind of
stressful,
huh?**

Our brain goes into emergency mode and works extra hard to look out for us.

It makes sure we figure out which are the people we can trust and where we can go to feel safe.

But then, after a while, when we've made new friends and know what to do, we don't have to be in emergency mode anymore.

Now imagine

if every day was like the
first day of school.

Constantly feeling
that stress and that fear over
and over again.

Always worried about
who will be your friend, or
who your teachers are, or
where your classroom is.

If you had that kind
of stress every day,

you'd be exhausted.

You probably wouldn't
be at your best.

And you might start to
overreact to small things.

That could look like...

suddenly not wanting to talk to your friends anymore.

getting into a fight with a friend who took your pencil without asking.

not being able to focus or pay attention in class.

That's how overwhelming experiences can change the brain.

OK.

Before we keep going, I want you
to try something real quick.

Find a piece of paper
and write your name.

Now write your name again
with your nondominant* hand.

Basically, if you're right-handed,
use your left one.

If you're a leftie (like me!),
use your right hand.

**Nondominant means the paired body part (in this case, the hand) you don't usually or naturally use.*

Not easy, is it?

It was probably uncomfortable and kind of slow, and you had to think about it a lot, right?*

*Unless you're ambidextrous, which is pretty cool. High-five!

But the more you practice writing
with your nondominant hand,
the better you'll get at it.

When you do this, your body
is learning and changing.

Your brain can do that too!

You see, the brain is like a muscle.

So just like you work out
your *muscles* to build strength
and get better at writing with
your nondominant hand, you
can work out your *brain* to get
better at managing stress and
heal from the effects of trauma.

One way to do this is
with physical exercise.

Remember when I told you that moving our bodies helps calm down our brains and helps us learn?

Well, it also makes sure we don't overreact to stress.

Well, I'm going to try
explaining that to you now.

Take a moment to close your eyes
and put your hand over your chest.

Count the beats of your heart and
feel the rhythm of your pulse.

That rhythm is naturally
comforting to us and
makes us feel safe.

You feel safe whenever
you do things that are like
a heartbeat—things that are
patterned, repetitive, and rhythmic.

This is important because
when our brains are safe and
calm, we can start to heal.

And guess what?

You do things that are patterned, repetitive, and rhythmic all the time!

Like:

WALKING, JUGGLING, RUNNING, RIDING A BIKE, SWIMMING, ROWING A BOAT, DRUMMING, JUMPING ROPE, KICKING A BALL AGAINST A WALL, DRIBBLING A BASKETBALL, PLAYING CATCH, DANCING,

AND SO MANY MORE!

All of these activities can help reset our brains and get us out of emergency mode.

We can also help our brains
by connecting with people.

Like friends,

family,

coaches,

teachers,

or a grownup

you trust.

Good experiences with the people you love and care about are more powerful than bad experiences.

But sometimes, we need an expert to help us figure out the best way to get better.

That's OK too!

No one asks to have something traumatic happen to them.

And our bodies and brains feel the impact when these things happen.

It's normal

for us (or for the people we know) to not always be able to control how we act when we have a lot going on in our lives.

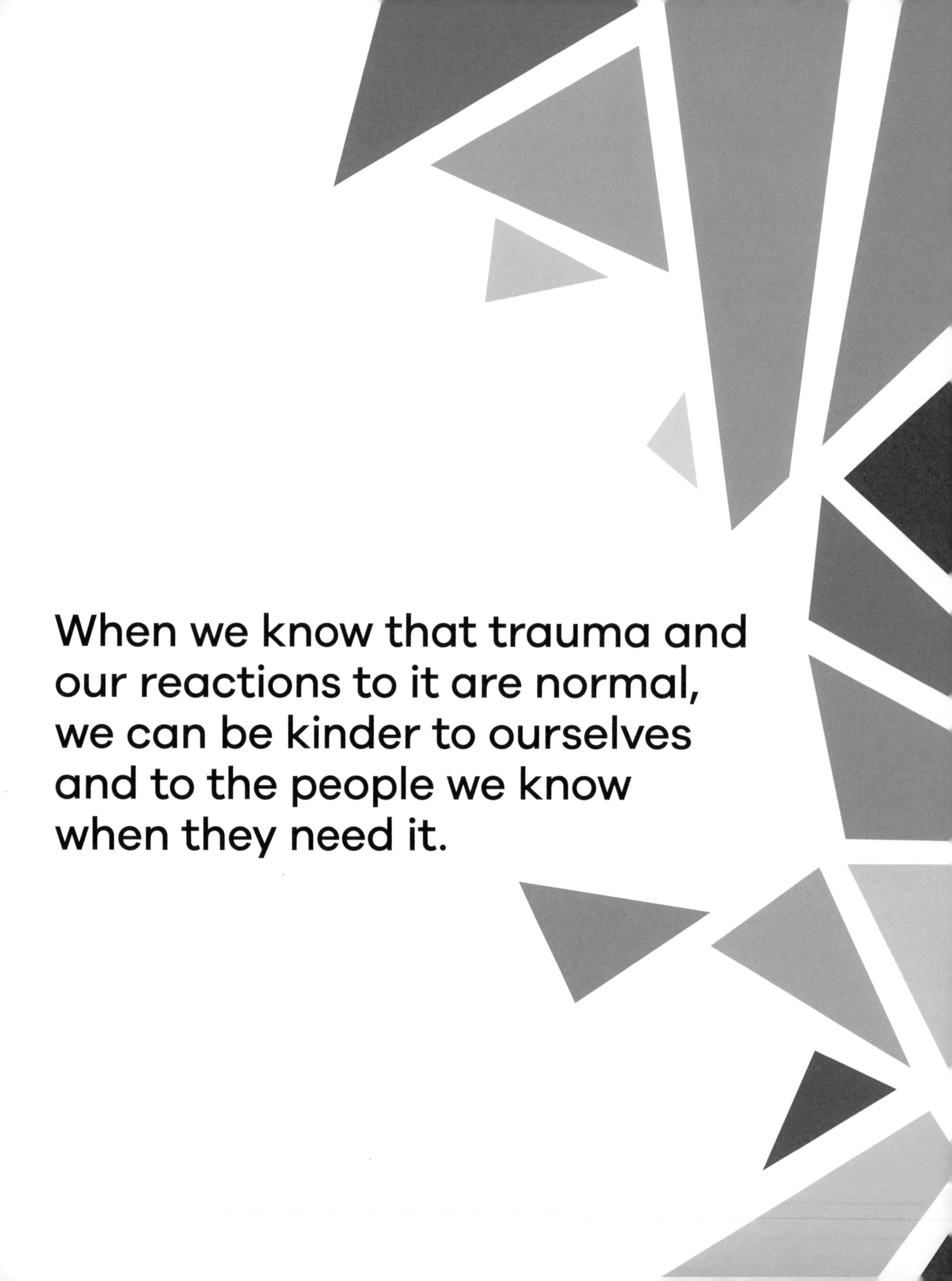

When we know that trauma and our reactions to it are normal, we can be kinder to ourselves and to the people we know when they need it.

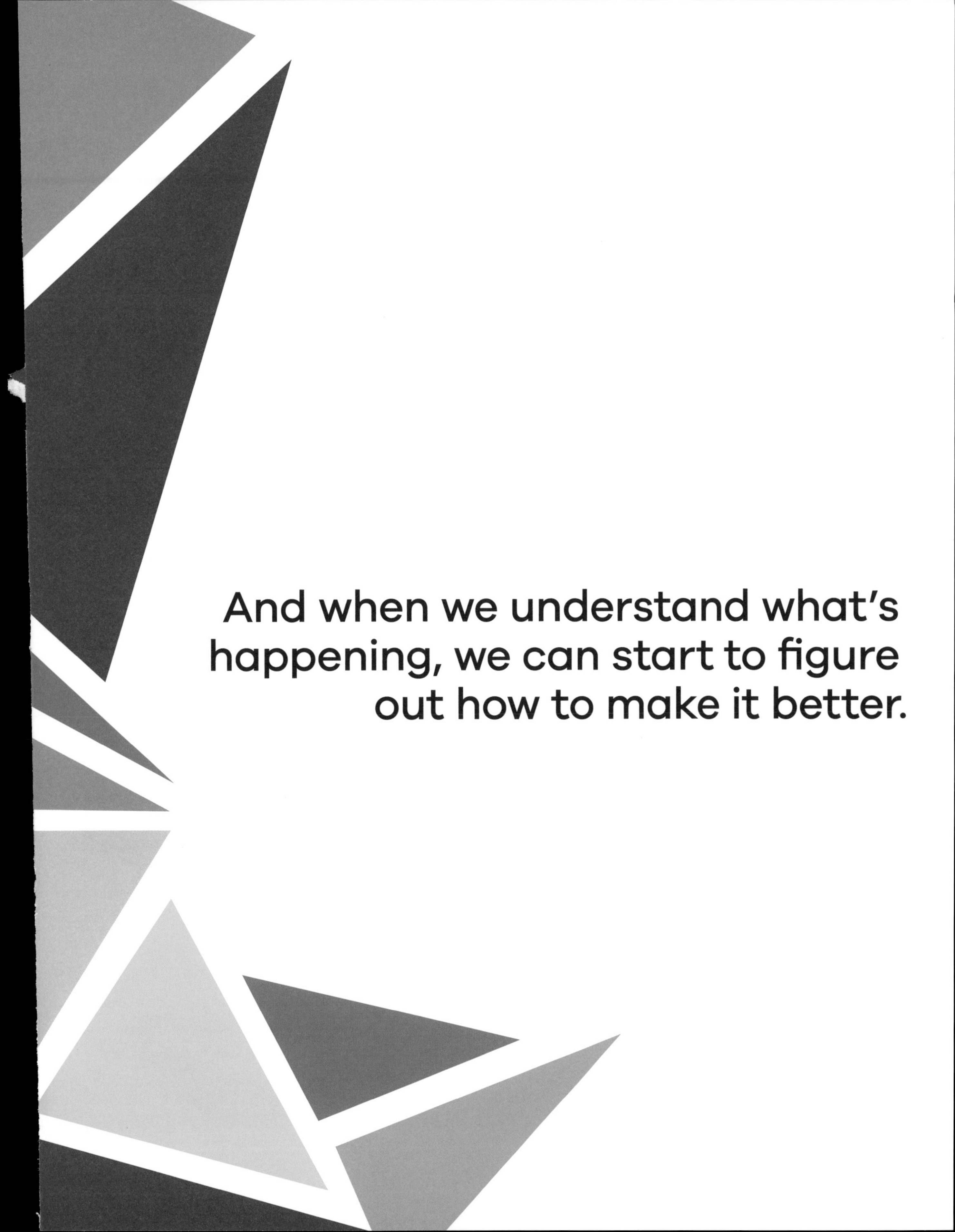

And when we understand what's happening, we can start to figure out how to make it better.

BECAUSE WE CAN

Outro

Feel like a healer yet? Or, at least, feel like you can be part of the team that helps a kid heal? I hope so.

For me, once I saw the world through the lens of trauma, I could never unsee it. It made me ask new questions and try new strategies for supporting kids—ones that were full of connection and movement. It also made me ask new questions and try new strategies for supporting myself. And, take it from me grownups, that's maybe the most important lesson here. You can't give what you don't have.

You can't be kinder and more understanding to someone impacted by trauma until you're kinder and more understanding to yourself. You can't provide the relational health a kid needs until you are relationally healthy.

So move **YOUR** body and connect with **YOUR** people.

So you can help a kid do the same.